STRESS RELIEF

MADE SIMPLE

Sue George

Haldane Mason

First published in the UK in 2000 by
Haldane Mason Ltd
59 Chepstow Road
London W2 5BP

Reprinted with revisions 2001

Box Set – ISBN: 1-902463-18-8
Book – ISBN: 1-902463-61-7

A HALDANE MASON BOOK

Editors: Jean Coppendale, Jillian Stewart, Beck Ward
Design: Louise Millar

Colour reproduction by CK Litho Ltd, UK

Printed in China

Picture Acknowledgements
Iain Bagwell: 57; Sue Ford: 7, 35, 38, 42–44, 54–55, 60; Amanda Heywood: 25, 50, 52; Joff Lee: 53; Andrew Sydenham: 1, 11, 15, 23, 25, 27, 29, 30, 32, 47, 57, 58–59; Image Bank: /Frans Lemmens: 9; /Britt Erlanson: 13, 39; John Kelly: 21; /Simon Wilkinson: 36; /Paolo Curto: 41; /Kaz Mori: 45; Tony Stone Images: /Dan Bosler: 17

Contents

Stress

Introduction

One of the biggest complaints people have these days is that they are stressed. And it isn't surprising – our lives seem to be relentlessly hectic and demanding.

Of course, a certain amount of stress is essential simply in order to get us out of bed in the mornings, but have too much, and we can almost cease to function. You can see this in the illustration below: the left of the diagram indicates how you feel when there is not enough stress in your life. A little more stress and you will start to feel better. When you are at the top of the curve you feel great … but too much stress and you start to feel worse again.

Some stress can be good for you – learn to gauge your stress levels with this curve.

Adapted from Clarke & Palmer, 1994.

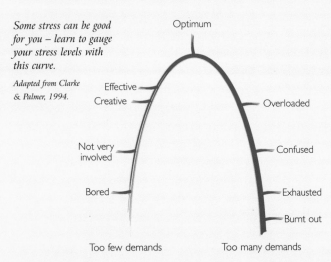

The problem is that our bodies have been designed with a 'fight or flight' response. In primitive times, human beings had to act very quickly when they saw danger coming; adrenaline flooded the body, in order to aid speedy reactions. Of course, this hasn't changed, so although the danger nowadays may only be whether or not we get to work on time, our bodies are still full of adrenaline, leaving us open to a whole range of stress-related symptoms.

4

HOW STRESSED ARE YOU?

There are many ways to combat stress, but first of all, look at this checklist to see whether you are over-stressed. Tick each one that applies to you.

Psychological symptoms:

- a sinking feeling that won't go away
- short temper and irritability
- waking up worrying
- thinking or talking about your problems all the time
- lack of sexual desire
- feelings of loneliness and isolation
- inability to make decisions
- inability to relax
- feelings of low-grade misery
- constant sense of frustration

Physical symptoms:

- drinking or smoking more than usual
- pains in the neck
- tension headaches, aches and pains
- loss of appetite
- stomach upsets
- grinding your teeth
- indigestion
- constant exhaustion
- sleeping a lot more or less than usual
- palpitations

Now count your ticks.

0–6 You are coping well at present, but make sure you know how to cope with stress at those times when problems arise.

7–12 Stress is starting to get to you, and you need to know how to relax. Make time for yourself to discover, by reading this book, what you need to do to feel better.

13+ Your stress levels are far too high and your lifestyle needs to change. Remember that stress can seriously damage your health. You should consider visiting your family doctor or complementary practitioner to find out what can be done to help.

All

IN THE

This first section looks at how you can make yourself the sort of person who can withstand stress – whatever is going on in your life. It shows how you can do this by:

- thinking positively and taking a proactive stance towards your problems
- looking at your habitual thought patterns and seeing whether they serve you well
- raising your self-esteem
- using meditation, visualization and affirmations
- coping with the stresses that change may bring

Mind?

Positive benefits

It's undoubtedly true that some people cope with stress a lot better than others. There's also great variation in how much stress one person wants in their life compared with someone else: some people like things to be hectic and demanding; others prefer lots of peace and quiet. Unfortunately, we don't always have total control over the stress levels in our lives, but we can change the way we think in order to improve our ability to cope with them.

The first and most important change we can make is to cultivate a positive and optimistic view of life. It may sound like no more than common sense but positive thinking and optimism mean you enjoy life a whole lot more. Optimists, by expecting the best, tend to do better than pessimists. Thinking that you can succeed in any given situation is obviously a better strategy than pessimism, where you convince yourself that you are in a no-win situation. It's a self-fulfilling prophecy – if you think you can't do something, you probably won't be able to.

MAKE A CHANGE

Start by actively deciding to be more cheerful and try not to moan or complain all the time. Remember the positive things in your life and focus on the good times and good memories you have experienced during the times when you feel down. Avoid dwelling on the negative but, if you do catch

yourself becoming negative, don't condemn yourself – just let it pass. Positive thinking may need practising and practice makes perfect.

Everyone has problems but positive people tend to react positively to their predicaments and use their difficulties to make improvements in their lives. You may not be able to solve a particular problem, but you can control your reaction to it. Feeling that you are able to take control over your life and taking responsibility for trying to solve your problems will make you feel less of a victim. Say you have been made redundant. This is, of course, a stressful situation for most people, but try looking at what your next step might be. Focus on job-hunting, rather than being consumed with anger. Contact your bank, mortgage and utility companies and any creditors and explain your situation. Use any spare time to keep exercising and stay fit and focused.

LEARNING TO ACCEPT

Many of us spend lots of time and energy worrying – but what's the point? Try to calm down your 'self-talk' – these are the constant conversations which run around your head and contribute to your stress. Use the energy you could spend worrying to figure out a range of solutions to your problem.

You need to accept that some situations cannot be changed – at least in the short term. Refuse to let them blight your life and focus, instead, on things that can be changed. This may seem difficult when you are faced with a mountain of worries – but it is possible to do.

In the struggle to stay positive, aim to focus on the good things you have.

A walk in the country can help to lift your spirits and clarify your thoughts.

Good thinking!

The way you think about your life, as well as the beliefs you hold about the world and other people, will have a profound effect on how much stress you have to face.

Many people have attitudes which actually add to their stress levels, although many of them do not realize it. These thoughts are referred to by psychologists as thinking errors.

NEGATIVE THINKING

Thinking about things in an unhelpful way can help cause stress – this can be a habit we fall into when we are already feeling stressed. The first step is to recognize whether you use any of these patterns habitually. If you do, consider whether they are really helping you:

1 Looking at things negatively: 'It'll never work.'

2 Mind-reading: 'My partner was home really late last night. She must be having an affair.'

3 Self-blame – blaming yourself for things over which you have no control: 'My brother's marriage broke up and I couldn't help him. I am a failure.'

4 Predicting: 'My new boss is bound to be an ogre because she got to the top so quickly.'

5 Labelling: 'I am such an idiot. I can never get things right.'

POSITIVE THINKING

If you now try to change these messages into positive ones, you may be surprised at how much less stressed you feel. You don't have to conquer all your feelings in one day – a little at a time is the best method and they will seem much more manageable. Try the following:

1 Looking at things positively: 'Let's see what would work instead.'

2 Finding out the facts: 'I'll ask my partner why she was so late last night. I'm sure there's a good reason.'

3 Allowing others to take responsibility: 'My brother's marriage broke up but that's his concern. I'll ask him if he needs my support now.'

4 Holding fire: 'My new boss got to the top very quickly. I'm sure I'll have a lot to learn from her.'

5 Acceptance: 'Everyone makes mistakes sometimes – I'm no different.'

Even the way you talk to yourself can compound your stress. Using words such as 'dreadful' and 'terrible' can make your situation seem more difficult than it actually is. In order to minimize the negative emotions attached to a situation, try 'not so good' or 'could be better'. Rather than thinking 'I'll die if I don't finish that report', try 'I'll finish that report as soon as I can'. This is called reframing – a technique used by some psychologists to get people to look at their problems in a different way. This essentially means changing your attitude to events by looking at them from a fresh perspective. For instance, you may be constantly annoyed and irritated that your house is always in a mess. You could reframe this by thinking that you have a busy and happy family who are always doing things together. A house which was always tidy would be one without the people you love most.

Take an afternoon out to organize your office space. This will dramatically reduce your stress levels and make things much easier to find.

How do you feel?

Many of our inner stresses come from low self-esteem. Feeling that we are somehow 'not good enough' may have come from our family, who never really accept us as we are.

Unrealistic expectations also lower self-esteem. If you decide that you must be married by the age of 30 and, by 29, you are not even dating, you will feel like a failure. You will not value your achievements and experiences, your relationships, or yourself as a person. One part of your life has not worked out exactly as planned and therefore you feel like a total failure.

Everyone prefers it when things go well, but often it's not possible to have every part of your life under control; things don't always work out as planned. Try setting yourself some realistic goals to achieve.

Imagine that someone is giving your funeral address: what would you like them to say about you, what do you want to have achieved over your life? Then work backwards to see how it might be possible to achieve it. This makes you proactive, rather than just reactive, and makes seemingly impossible dreams more realistic.

Putting things down on paper makes them seem much more concrete. Be as specific as possible, then you will be able to see the next step to take. But make each individual goal realistic, or you will set yourself up for failure – and increased stress.

BODY IMAGE

One of the ways low self-esteem operates more forcibly for women (and – increasingly – for men) is in our attitude towards our bodies. It can be very difficult to consider ourselves attractive when we are not young, slim and athletic. Nothing we can do to improve our appearance will ever be enough and our negative feelings about ourselves are compounded by unrealistic images in magazines, and so on.

Yet, as we know deep down, the look of the supermodel is totally artificial, dependent on the right lighting, clothes and make-up. Self-acceptance, valuing yourself for all that you are, is a goal, but there are also practical things you can do. Don't focus on losing weight; beauty comes in all shapes and sizes. Instead make sure that you eat healthily and keep fit; using some of the sections in this book on diet and exercise will help.

Quieten your mind

In order to lessen some of the mental stresses you may feel, a spiritual practice such as meditation can be very beneficial. It helps you gain greater peace, balance and focus and has the practical effect of helping you transcend the demands and difficulties of daily life. Meditation can calm you down, lower blood pressure, improve concentration and energy, as well as reduce pulse rate and adrenaline.

For your first attempt at meditation, sit in a chair with an upright back (such as a dining chair). Keep your feet on the ground and your arms resting on your legs; place the backs of your hands on your knees. Hold your thumb and first finger together.

Become aware of your breathing. When you breathe out speak a word – many people use the word *Om*. Concentrate on your breathing and the sound of the word. When you are ready to finish, stop speaking the word; sit silently for a few more minutes before you get up. For best results, practise morning and evening.

The other less spiritually focused method of meditation uses guided visualization. Imagine yourself walking to the most peaceful, beautiful place you can think of. It might be a calm country meadow, a river-bank, or a seashore. The weather is perfect, and you feel totally relaxed and at peace with the world. Notice the sights,

sounds and scents you come across. Enjoy the feeling of peace both inside and outside your body.

Turn to your spiritual side for relaxation and clarity of thought after a stressful day.

AFFIRMATIONS

Affirmations are short statements about yourself or your life that you want to change. Write them down, putting them where they may be seen easily: on the fridge, notice board or a computer screen saver. By writing them down, you imprint a positive message on your subconscious. Keep them in the present tense and always use positive language, not negative language. So not: 'I am now losing weight', but: 'I am the size that's right for me'.

But you don't just have to always rely on yourself for help with positive statements: if you have particular worries or issues you want to deal with, such as gaining confidence, stopping smoking, or enjoying better sex, or you want help to relax, self-hypnosis tapes can be very useful. They use affirmations spoken under soothing foreground music which act on your subconscious brain, even though you don't consciously hear them. Ask your doctor or complementary practitioner for help in selecting a tape that is right for your needs.

All change

Too much change at once is one of the most common ways people become stressed. Some changes may be pleasant, of course, such as getting married or achieving success at work. Too many all at once, however, may tip your stress balance. If you want to make big changes to your life, such as splitting up with a partner or taking on a mortgage, you will cut down on the potential stress if you plan as much as possible in advance.

Some situations, however, would challenge anyone to stay calm, such as illness, redundancy, the sudden departure of a partner – leaving you a single parent, or the death of a loved one. Your sense of security and of how your life should be balanced suddenly vanish, leaving pain, powerlessness and a sense of loss. But it is often the most difficult situations which, in the long term, will make you grow and gain in personal power.

When things are at their toughest, take the situation one day at a time. Accept your losses and be grateful for what you have had. Recognize that although it may not feel that way, you are actually coping really well. Get support from others and include professionals when appropriate. Some difficult or awkward changes can be improved by your own actions. If you lose your job, you can get another one, but other events, such as the death of a parent, will mark you forever.

Getting in touch with your spiritual side can help – whether or not you have any religious beliefs, developing a connection with nature and the rest of the human race can help. And always remember: this too will pass.

Borage is particularly useful as a herbal remedy for worry and depression.

15

Behaviour

Pat

Now we consider how changing the way you behave can help you reduce the amount of stress in your life. You can do this by:

- getting organized in all areas of your life
- developing warm, supportive relationships
- acting assertively rather than passively or aggressively
- making time for play rather than succumbing to workaholism

terns

Let's get organized

Good planning is one of the most effective ways of avoiding situations which cause stress. Organizing things in advance also means that you will be able to improve your quality of life. Here's how to improve your organizational techniques in some key areas.

MONEY MANAGEMENT

One of the surest ways of becoming very stressed is to have no control over your finances. Of course, the best way to be in control is to always live within your means. Work out a budget: figure out exactly how much you need for essentials such as rent, mortgage and bills then you can see how much you have left for fun.

These days, however, it is very common to owe a great deal of money, particularly on credit cards. Lenders don't really care whether or not you can afford to borrow – until the day comes when you can't afford the minimum repayments.

Of course, the best solution is not to get into debt in the first place. But if you are, then make sure you act before the situation becomes unmanageable – even if you have to cut up your credit cards so you can't use them. If your spending is out of control, you may find it helpful to visit a debt counselling centre.

TIME MANAGEMENT

Trying to do everything, rushed off your feet at work and home? So is everyone else. Welcome to a world designed for maximum stress. Manage your time carefully and remember:

- Everything takes a lot longer than you think it will; add contingency time to allow for delays.
- Plan your day in advance, preferably the day before.
- Make good use of your diary, balancing work with other parts of your life.
- Don't take on too much and delegate where possible.
- Manage your energy levels – if you are too tired, stop what you are doing.
- Time spent slumped in front of the TV is lost and does not really contribute positively to your life in any way.
- Don't expect too much of yourself or anyone else – not everything has to be perfect.

CLUTTER

Many people have homes which are full of stuff that they don't really want. They hoard old letters, bits of string, clothes they no longer wear. Clutter equals stress, and if you have too much of it, you might start to have problems finding what you need. It also takes time because you may have to clean it and organize it.

To solve your clutter problems, think about how you feel when you've cleaned out some cupboards. You probably feel totally refreshed with a sense of achievement. So throw or give away all the things you don't love, or have a good use for. Then organize what is left. You will save time and effort on a daily basis.

HOME

Start going through your home, room by room, sorting out clutter – unwanted presents, out-of-date telephone directories, empty bottles, ancient newspapers, plastic bags, food past its sell-by date, old coat-hangers, out-of-date reference books, underwear that long ago gave up the ghost, old shoes and wellington boots, cardboard boxes, radios that don't work, empty or broken pens, dead house plants, broken flowerpots and all the rest of the junk you were holding onto just in case…

Ask yourself as you go from cupboard to cupboard: is it decorative? Is it functional? If it's neither, bin it. Try getting out all your clothes and sort them into four big piles:

- definitely want to keep
- so old it can only be worn for gardening or go in the bin
- not sure – needs a second look – give it to charity if you're really not going to use it
- needs attention – dry-cleaning, washing, mending or altering

WORK

- make your environment pleasant with plants and pictures
- clean the windows, your computer keyboard and screen
- check or service your tools
- update your contacts/address book.
- sort out all papers – either throw them away, deal with them or file them

Once you have done all this – reward yourself. You'll probably need a bath after pottering about in all that dust – so take it, add some aromatic oils and enjoy that feeling of peace and being in control.

Good support

'No man is an island', as John Dunne wrote, and no man or woman can successfully lower their stress levels without involving other people from time to time. Relationships of all sorts, but particularly romantic relationships, can be a cause of stress; but conversely, they can also help relieve stress.

Close friendships are commonly accepted as one of the reasons why women suffer fewer mental health problems than men after the breakdown of partnerships. While men tend to rely on themselves, women rely more on the help of others. Female friends tend to be much better at reciprocal support in both practical and emotional ways. It's clear that good friends are incredibly important.

You don't have to put on an act and they can also help you laugh at life and yourself. Don't let friends go just because your partner, children or work take priority. And don't take them for granted either – friendships need work. Even a phone call or e-mail is better than nothing.

When a particular problem is causing you excessive stress, joining a support group can be useful. Talking about shared issues with like-minded people can be of great help: they are going through similar things to you and you need not be afraid of jeopardizing your friendships or relying on friends too much.

Family life can sometimes be stressful and, as anyone who's been there will know, being a parent of small children can be tremendously hard work, as well as a great joy. Good organization can help here: where possible, delegate housework and similar tasks to your partner, to older children or to paid help. Get babysitters so you can still go out from time to time. Ask your friends and family for help when you need it.

Don't have expectations which are too high. Accept that there will be the inevitable juggling but cut down on anything that you can – and enjoy it while it lasts!

Romantic relationships and partnerships often suffer when one person is under a lot of stress. Snapping at your partner, withdrawing emotionally and losing interest in sex are just some of the possible effects. Sometimes, your partner can suffer just as much as you, but it is always hard to see someone else's needs and worries when yours seem to be so important and apparent.

Making time for yourself and your loved ones is an essential part of a stress-free life – don't underestimate the power of relaxation and fun!

Try these ways of helping your relationship withstand stress:
- Make time for your partner – especially if you have children.
- Take up a hobby together.
- Talk over problems and listen to what your partner has to say.
- Take care how you criticize your partner: don't nag or attack.
- Share responsibility for whether your relationship works; don't simply expect your partner to make you happy.
- Value your own space, interests and friendships too.

Assert yourself

How many times have you said to yourself: 'I'm doing too much, why can't someone else help'? Or wished that you could say to your boss: 'My workload is too great. I need to leave on time more often'. You need to increase your ability to be assertive.

Assertiveness is not aggression: it simply means stating what you want yourself and, in turn, listening to how other people think and feel. If you become honest about what you want, others have to be honest with you. It means no one feels taken advantage of and everyone has a chance of achieving their needs.

When you are considering a particular situation where you will need to be assertive, first think about what you want. You will need to state how you feel, listen to the other person's point of view, and be prepared to compromise. Recognize that others have their needs and opinions that should be respected – but ensure that their needs do not outweigh yours.

Learn to say no and don't be forced into doing things you don't want to do. Use the broken record technique. Keep repeating yourself if they don't take any notice, or react in manipulative ways. For instance, you may say to your sister: 'I don't want to babysit for you this weekend.' She may reply: 'Well, I won't be able to go

out then.' But you are aware that you look after her children far more than she looks after yours, so simply say: 'I know that, but I still don't want to babysit for you this weekend.'

Stress is often related to people being unfairly demanding or generally unpleasant. Assertiveness can be very useful in this context. Be specific and state your feelings, rather than attacking the other person. You can defuse tension and help yourself, if you ask for constructive criticism. Don't accept that your work, for example, is terrible. Ask them what exactly is wrong about your work, and how you could improve it.

People who put you down can make you feel insecure and worthless. Assertiveness, however, can help build self-esteem. Fight the impulse to try and match their spiteful comments. Try to realize that it is their own insecurities that make them behave in such a way and, if you feel their comments have some truth to them, ask them how you can make a change – they may be completely taken aback by your response.

Less work, more play

The modern world, with its culture of long hours and pressure, means that for more and more of us, work takes over our lives. Working constantly doesn't mean that you work more effectively – quite the opposite.

People who work constantly, without balancing it with the rest of their lives, are setting themselves up to become greatly stressed. Those who work more than about 45 hours a week make more mistakes, get sick more easily, and suffer from a range of physical problems such as backache or headaches.

Some people, however, have chosen to be workaholics, and are looking for ways to escape from the other parts of their lives. They want to avoid difficult situations at home or fill their lives that otherwise are empty and lonely. If this is the case with you, try to figure out how to cope with your real problems.

The best way to cope with work-related stress is to counterbalance it with a good dose of play. Step outside your usual routine: choose hobbies that are very different from your work. Don't just vegetate in front of the television when you get home, do things that are truly relaxing. Try learning a language, or go to a creative writing class. In one study, dancing, specifically dances that involved learning particular routines, such as salsa or Scottish reels, was shown to be the best way of all to increase positive feelings. Most important of all – get out and have some fun.

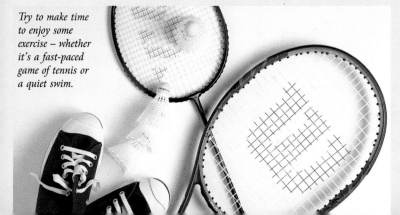

Try to make time to enjoy some exercise – whether it's a fast-paced game of tennis or a quiet swim.

23

You are

WHAT

In this section we take a look at the role of food and how eating well can help you avoid, and withstand, stress. Here we explain:

- what constitutes healthy eating
- why some foods raise your energy levels and some bring it down
- which supplements can help relieve stress
- how to stop smoking and drinking too much alcohol or caffeine
- how a simple detox plan can make you feel great

you eat

Healthy eating

Thanks to years of information by health educators, many of us know the theory of what constitutes healthy eating. To make ourselves physically able to withstand stress, as well as remain in the best of health, the most important thing is to eat a balanced diet.

What does this mean in practice? First, you need to eat five servings of carbohydrates a day, preferably wholegrains which contain zinc and B vitamins, amongst others. White bread, rice and pasta can provide slow-release energy but have less fibre to aid digestion.

Don't be scared of fat – a certain amount is essential in your diet. Use olive oil in place of margarine and butter, wherever possible. Try not to eat specially produced low-fat foods; just eat small quantities of the full-fat equivalent. The best way of helping your body to use fat is to eat a similar amount of fibre at the same time – so have biscuits with your cheese.

Try to eat some dairy produce each day in order to provide calcium for healthy teeth and bones. If you follow a non-dairy diet, other calcium-rich foods include tofu, figs, canned fish and dark green leafy vegetables.

Protein is also essential to repair our body tissue, build muscles, strengthen our immune systems and give the brain serotonin, which keeps us happy. Chicken is a versatile and fairly healthy choice or, for non-meat eaters, try eggs, nuts or cooked lentils.

The antioxidant vitamins A, C and E are essential for good health and for fighting the free radicals which are implicated in many different serious diseases, especially cancer. A good stock of fruit and vegetables should supply you with all you need. Although the scientific world still isn't really united on this issue, vitamin supplements are probably not absolutely necessary if you eat a varied range of fresh foods.

EAT YOUR GREENS, REDS AND YELLOWS

Try to eat five portions of fruit and vegetables a day. Some nutritionists say that the best way to ensure you get all the vitamins and minerals you need is to ensure you eat produce from the whole range of food colours. Have red, yellow and green peppers, beetroot, carrots, broccoli and leaves such as rocket and raw spinach. These five portions are in addition to any potatoes, which count as carbohydrate.

Increase your fruit and vegetable consumption – and hardly notice it:

- buy fruit and vegetable smoothies in your local sandwich bar
- invest in a juicer; freshly squeezed juices retain all their vitamins
- buy lots of vegetables and blend them into a delicious soup
- register with an organic vegetables delivery box scheme – fresh vegetables are delivered to your doorstep every week
- have a salad once a day

Energy ups and downs

Are you eating things which, unknown to you, are depleting your body's energy reserves? Replace them with foods and habits which will make you feel good.

ENERGY

The human body is not designed to eat really large meals – we should be grazing on smaller amounts during the day. Large meals put a strain on the digestive system and make us sleepy. Fresh fruit and vegetables have a high level of vitamins and minerals. Buy organic produce if possible, as it hasn't been treated with potentially harmful pesticides and fertilizers. Try: spinach, apples, bananas and asparagus.

FIBRE

Fibre is essential to counteract stress-related digestive problems such as diarrhoea and constipation. Try to start your day with something like low-fat, high-fibre muesli and fruit.

AVOIDING MEALS

Sometimes, too much stress can make us avoid eating altogether. Our stomachs feel churned up and we have far too much to do to consider food. But not eating depletes our energy reserves and nutrient stores, such as potassium, iron and zinc, which help us to feel good. Try: sardines on toast and plenty of fruit.

FATTY FOODS

While crisps, chips, full-fat cheese, cakes and pastries taste delicious, they contain empty calories. They make you fat – a source of stress in itself – without giving you any nutrients, and may put a strain on your cardio-vascular system. Fat is needed for good health, but should be from food such as fish, or olive and nut oils.

ENJOYABLE MEALTIMES

Eat slowly, chew well and aim to make your mealtimes an opportunity to relax or a shared experience with others.

TAKE IT AWAY

It feels as if sugar gives you a boost, but sugar is one of the greatest energy-robbers there is. When you eat refined sugar added to food, your blood sugar levels rush up and you feel great. Shortly after, however, they plummet, leaving you feeling more tired than before. Instead of eating sugary food, try fruit or pasta which contain fibre and slow-release sugar.

Try filling up on vitamin-rich vegetables or fruit rather than biscuits or sweets.

Stress-fighting supplements

Sometimes our bodies need a little help in staying calm, increasing their energy levels, boosting their immune systems and so on. Before turning to sleeping tablets, or going to the doctor because you think you need tranquillizers or anti-depressants, try some of the following. These dietary aids are also helpful in preventing physical and psychological problems. If you are taking any prescribed medicines, ask your doctor before adding supplements, as some react negatively with them.

CO-ENZYME Q-10

Q-10 enables the body's cells to release energy from food, making you feel as if you have more get up and go. The body creates Q-10 itself, but illness, ageing and stress reduce its production.

ECHINACEA

This herb is commonly used to boost the immune system and help the body fight colds and flu. Also useful for skin problems such as eczema which can be exacerbated by stress.

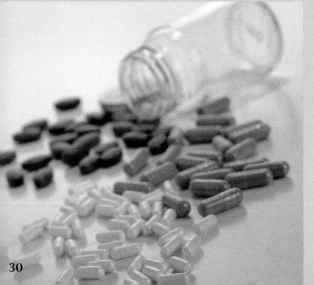

Most herbal supplements are available in handy tablet form.

EVENING PRIMROSE OIL

This is very popular for treating many hormonal conditions in women, such as PMS and sore breasts.

GINKGO BILOBA

Improves concentration by stimulating the blood supply to the brain, and may help to slow down the ageing process. Scientists have recently discovered that ginseng and ginkgo biloba taken together can be particularly beneficial to our mental and intellectual performance. Specifically, they may help with short-term demanding situations such as passing exams or giving presentations at work. Available as a tea and tincture, amongst others.

GINSENG

Used in China for over 5,000 years, ginseng is a root extract which can greatly enhance memory as well as acting as a general tonic. It also stimulates energy in all parts of the body and can aid digestion. Avoid taking if you are generally feeling unwell, during pregnancy or with tea and coffee. Available in tablets, tinctures and powders.

GUARANA

This herb revitalizes the mind and body and makes you feel generally energetic – partly because its seeds contain a small amount of caffeine.

KAVA-KAVA

An anti-anxiety herbal remedy, Kava-kava creates a positive sense of well-being and relaxation, rather as though you've had a couple of glasses of wine, but without the related side-effects!

KOMBUCHA

Kombucha is a fungus and has been used as a tea for thousands of years. It contains many vitamins and minerals and helps boost the immune system.

ROYAL JELLY

This is the natural food of the queen bee. It is said to improve general well-being, boost the immune system, and increase stamina and energy.

ST JOHN'S WORT

Becoming increasingly popular as a treatment for mild depression, St John's Wort is a yellow-flowered plant. In Germany, it is successfully prescribed instead of conventional anti-depressants and as a restorative tonic for the nervous system. Tablets are available in a number of different strengths and also as a tea.

VERVAIN

This herb helps stress-induced illnesses and depression and is commonly used as a relaxant tonic. Avoid during pregnancy. Vervain is available in many forms, including tea and herbal tablets.

Bad-habit busters

Smoking and drinking alcohol or caffeine are three of the things people do most often to cope with stress. Sometimes, a simple drink or two can be more worrying as these habits become addictions. It may feel as if smoking and drinking are reducing your stress levels. In the long and even medium term, however, they actually make you feel more stressed.

SMOKING

Many people use smoking as a coping mechanism but, of course, everyone knows that its long-term harmful effects far outweigh what seem to be its short-term benefits. It is known that smoking can cause cancer and heart disease. What most smokers really want to know is how to give up: Try:

- nicotine gum or patches
- behavioural counselling to find strategies for avoiding situations when you want to smoke
- acupuncture
- will power – the oldest method of stopping smoking and still essential

Smoking: only a short-term 'solution' to stress, and certainly not the healthiest one.

ALCOHOL

A quick trip to a pub or bar after a hard day may seem just what's needed but reliance on alcohol can cause more problems than it solves. It can hinder mental performance, drain the body of nutrients, make us put on weight through its empty calories and stop us sleeping well.

While we may want to believe that alcohol is actually good for us, medical evidence does not really support that theory. What is known is that a small amount of red wine may help reduce cardiovascular disease – but only in middle-aged men and post-menopausal women. Try:

- not to drink more than one alcoholic drink an hour; alternate with water
- to avoid drinking more than the recommended units of 21 units for men and 14 for women per week
- not to binge drink
- to have one or two alcohol-free days a week

CAFFEINE

As with sugar, caffeine lifts your energy and then makes it drop again. Coffee, tea, colas and chocolate all contain caffeine. Too much caffeine increases blood pressure, gives you headaches and palpitations and increases tension.

There is no reason to remove caffeine from your diet completely, but, if you tend to drink more than 2–3 cups of caffeinated drinks a day, you need to find ways to cut down. Why not try:

- replacing tea, coffee or cola with herb teas or water
- going for a walk outside or opening a window if you feel sleepy
- gradually mixing decaffeinated tea and coffee with caffeinated beverages

EASY DETOXING

Getting rid of the toxins in your body can help a great deal to improve your energy levels. The way to do this is to 'detox' – cut back on foods that are known to generate toxins.

There are many different detox plans around, some of them much stricter than others. If you are a novice at detoxing, however, don't demand too much of yourself. While some plans require that you spend the weekend eating only fruit, or drinking water and herb tea without eating anything, this should not be done without medical advice. Instead, over the course of a fortnight, try this easy-to-stomach detox plan; it can be particularly helpful if you have been overindulging:

- Don't drink tea, coffee or fizzy drinks; avoid all alcohol and replace with herb teas, particularly vervain, chamomile, green tea or fresh mint.
- Drink at least two litres of water a day; many people drink far too little water and are chronically dehydrated; in addition, while you are detoxing, you will need plenty of water to flush the toxins out of your body.
- During this fortnight, the majority of what you eat should be fruit and vegetables.
- Good detox vegetables include spinach, tomatoes, peppers, radishes, watercress, broccoli and beetroot.
- When you are peckish, eat a piece of fruit, but only eat one banana a day; apricots, kiwi fruits, oranges and raspberries are good detoxing fruits.
- Avoid red meat – lean chicken breast is fine, but you should only eat meat or fish once a day.
- Avoid white bread, rice and pasta – use wholegrains instead.

Exercise

TO FIGHT

*T*his section gives the low-down on the health and stress-relieving benefits of regular exercise. Exercise is one of the easiest ways of reducing stress – even in a really busy life it's worth finding the time for it. Begin by:

- answering our questionnaire and deciding which form of exercise is right for you
- using our home workout plan to keep fit without leaving the house
- getting a taste for yoga and trying these yoga asanas to help you de-stress
- finding out about other methods of stress-reducing exercise

Stress

Get fit, fight stress

Now that you have learned what you need to eat to stress-proof your body, it's time for the next step – exercise. Exercise has been proved to lower cholesterol levels, release muscle tension, increase the supply of oxygen to the body and brain, and improve cardiovascular function by strengthening and enlarging the heart.

Exercise is also an outlet for negative emotions such as frustration, anger and irritability – by releasing feel-good endorphins to the brain. Regular exercise also releases the amount of adrenal hormones the body produces in reaction to stress, as well as increasing your energy and fitness levels.

Exercise, therefore, should be a priority. But it's not true that if you don't go to the gym, you can't get fit; just remember that you need to balance aerobic exercise, such as running, cycling or swimming, preferably for at least 20 minutes three times a week, with exercises for strength and flexibility.

There are as many different exercise needs as there are people – and if you are exercising in ways that don't suit you, you won't be able to stick to your exercise plan.

FITNESS QUIZ

Try this quick quiz to see which sort of fitness plan is right for you.

What's your favourite way to relax?

a) in bars or clubs; you like to work hard/play hard

b) chatting with friends

c) with a hobby like gardening, reading or cinema-going

When you were at school, what was your attitude to sports?

a) you liked anything you were good at

b) you enjoyed team sports

c) you hated being made to do things

How important is it that you lose weight?

a) that's one of the reasons you want to exercise

b) you could lose a few pounds

c) you're fine as you are

How would you best describe your personality?

a) motivated, energetic

b) sociable, cheerful

c) you like doing your own thing

How do you like to feel after exercise?

a) as though you've been working hard

b) as though you've enjoyed yourself

c) that you've had a good workout, but you're not exhausted

How often do you exercise at present?

a) several times a week

b) when you get round to it

c) rarely

How many hours a week do you spend at work?

a) 50 or more

b) 40–49

c) under 40

Your attention span is:

a) good

b) all over the place

c) good – if you like what you're doing

How to score

Now count up your answers and see which category applies to you.

Mostly as: You want results – you're goal orientated and committed. The sort of person who'd most enjoy going to the gym.

Mostly bs: Sociability is very important to you, so join some classes. Make sure you balance the types of exercise – so go dancing with your partner, jogging with friends, play badminton with your sister.

Mostly cs: You're a real individual. Try yoga, swimming or home workouts. You don't want to rely on other people or try to fit into their schedules.

Home workout 1

You can have as good a workout at home as you can in a gym with a personal trainer, and you can do it at times that suit you. Do this workout as many times a week as you can – three to five times is ideal. As you get fitter, aim to increase the number of times you repeat each set of exercises. If something hurts suddenly or you feel dizzy, stop.

WARMING UP (5 minutes)

Before you start exercising, it's very important that you warm up properly. Walk on the spot for two minutes, then jog for another two.

STRETCHES (5 minutes)

Each set of muscles should be stretched to improve flexibility and avoid injury. Hold them for eight to ten seconds, then change sides and repeat.

Arm stretch: stretch each arm above your head, then bend it behind you from the elbow, pressing down with the other hand.

Chest stretch: stand facing forwards, reach behind you with one arm, and turn your body away from your arm. Feel the stretch across the front of your chest.

Thigh stretch 1: stretch the back of the thighs or hamstrings by performing the exercise on page 40.

Thigh stretch 2: stretch each thigh by balancing on one leg and bending the other at the knee. Hold your foot and count to ten. Keep the knee you're standing on relaxed.

This yoga posture – known as Parsvakonasana – *provides a good stretch for the legs, the hips and the sides of the trunk.*

CARDIOVASCULAR WORK
(20 minutes)

This is the part of the workout that exercises your heart and lungs. You are probably working hard enough if you are sweating lightly, and can talk, but are slightly out of breath.

If you want to lose weight, you'll need to do 45 minutes of aerobic exercise three times a week.

Vary your activity: you could try skipping, aerobic-style dancing, rebounding, or walking up and down the stairs. By doing this you will ensure that your interest in getting fit is maintained, encouraging you to keep going. These activities may be mixed with a few of the following simple exercises:

Squats: stand up, place your feet together and push your bottom back. As you do this, bend your legs as if you are going to sit down. Come back up again and repeat.

Dumbbell run: using dumbbells, or tin cans, move your arms as if you were running but keep your feet still. Try not to wobble about from side to side too much.

Lunges: with your hands on your hips, and your feet together, step forward with one leg, bending it as you go. Bring it back, and then repeat with the other leg.

MAXIMUM BENEFIT

During your workout, make sure that your heart is working at 70–80% of its capacity. Your maximum heart rate (number of heartbeats per minute) may be calculated easily by subtracting your age from 220.

Remember to take your pulse, on your wrist, during cardiovascular activity to make sure you are working at an appropriate rate for your body.

Home workout 2

Now you need to condition and tone the various different muscle groups. As much of this part of the workout takes place on the floor, it's a good idea to use an exercise mat or thick towel to cushion you. Try to repeat each move ten times or as many as is comfortable.

CONDITIONING
(10 minutes)
Half press-ups: keep your hands shoulder-width apart and balance on your knees. For full press-ups, keep your legs straight so that only your hands and toes touch the floor.

Stomach curls: lie on your back, with your knees bent and your feet apart. Raise your palms off the floor. Tuck your chin in to your chest, and raise your shoulders a few inches off the floor. Make sure that your lower back and pelvis stay on the floor.

Buttocks: lie on your back, with your knees bent and your feet apart. Keeping your shoulders on the floor, and without arching your back, lift your bottom off the floor by squeezing your buttocks together.

Waist: still on your back with your knees bent, stretch your arms out to your sides. Roll your head in one direction and your knees in the other. Then repeat in the opposite direction.

Thighs: sit up with your back straight and your legs stretched out in front of you. Place your hands on the floor. Lift one leg up about a foot (about 30 cm) in front of you, then slowly move it out to the side as far as is comfortable. Then move it back and down. Repeat with the other leg.

Outer thighs: lie on your side with your legs straight out. Lift the upper leg as far in the air as is comfortable, then bring it back down. Repeat 10 times, then change sides.

COOL DOWN
(5 minutes)
Now it's time to finish. Gently stretch your muscles as you did when you were warming up (see page 38). Finish the workout by walking on the spot for a few minutes to bring your body back to normal.

Stomach curls: keep your movements as smooth as possible. Jerking your body may lead to injury.

Yoga

Yoga has been practised in India for thousands of years and is now probably the most popular mind-body-spirit practice in the West, as well. Yoga techniques are deceptively simple and practising yoga regularly can be a highly effective stress reliever. Yoga will help you to stretch and tone your body, whilst also relieving physical and mental tension through breathing techniques and physical postures.

There are a various types of yoga you can study: *Hatha* is the most popular form practiced in the West, mixing physical 'asanas' or postures with breathing techniques. There are also more spiritual forms of yoga, such as *Kundalini* and *Raja*, and *Ashtanga* yoga, which is more physical and energetic.

Yoga is not a competitive form of exercise so don't try too hard. If your body tells you to stop or slow down, then listen; it's not a 'go for the burn' type of exercise.

Here are some simple asanas which will aid stress relief although, for best results, you should attend a regular yoga class which will include asanas to stretch every part of your body.

GOOD POSTURE (*tadasana*)

Stand straight up with your feet together, arms straight down by your sides. Let your shoulders relax downwards, shut your eyes and focus on your spine. Breathe calmly in this position for a few minutes.

FORWARD BEND
(*uttanasana*)

Stretches the legs and spine, relaxes heart and neck, de-stresses mind and body.

Stand straight with your arms at your sides, looking straight ahead. Inhale, raising your arms above your head. As you breathe out, bend at the hips. Bring your arms forward and down until you touch the floor. Then, either keep your hands touching the floor or have them clasping your ankles. Repeat five times.

To come out of the pose, curl upwards one vertebra at a time, bringing up the head from the chest as a final move.

SHOULDERSTAND
(*sarvangasana*)

Good for stomach muscles, strengthens upper back, helps blood circulation and induces relaxation.

Lie on your back and lift your legs in the air. With your elbows and lower arms on the ground, support your lower back with your hands. Your weight should be on your shoulders and upper back. Take five to ten deep breaths before slowly lowering your legs, keeping them very straight.

THE CORPSE (*savasana*)

This is the quintessential relaxing pose which usually takes place at the end of a yoga session. It calms and energizes the body and mind.

Lie on your back, with your feet slightly apart and your arms at your sides with palms facing upwards. Close your eyes and take a deep breath. Focus on a particular part of the body and tense it. Then relax. Do this for each part of your body. Then breathe deeply, concentrating on your breathing for a further 5–10 minutes.

Yoga 2

*After learning how to stand properly and relax, the first thing
a yoga student will learn is a set of asanas – such as this one,
known as* **Salute to the Sun.**

1 Stand upright, bringing your hands together with palms touching and fingers facing upwards.

2 Breathe in slowly and deeply, raising your arms above your head. Push backwards with your arms and arching your back. Breathe out in the same way, and bend forwards (as in the forward bend on page 43).

3 Breathe in and crouch down. With your knees still bent, slide your right leg back, keeping your left foot flat on the floor. Keep your palms on the floor, level with your left foot. Bend your head backwards. Breathe out.

4 Breathe in again, and move your left leg out to join the right. With your feet together lift your body off the floor, taking a position as though you were going to do press-ups. Keep your arms and legs straight.

5 Breathe out slowly, lowering your entire body onto the floor. Breathe in, bending your trunk backwards, leaving your stomach, pelvis and legs pressed to the floor.

6 Breathe out, lifting up your bottom and back to make an inverted 'V'. Your feet and hands should be flat on the floor.

7 Breathe in and leave your left leg stretched out. Step forward with your right leg and lift your head into the position of step 3.

8 Breathe out, dropping your arms. Repeat this series of asanas another 1–3 times.

Mind–body therapies

Other exercise-related techniques can also help you withstand stress and avoid the accumulation of tension in your body. To help you learn more efficiently, and avoid getting into bad habits, you will benefit from contacting a teacher or joining a group.

ALEXANDER TECHNIQUE
Involves realigning your body, teaching you how to improve your posture: the way you walk, how you sit at your desk and stand. Many of the physical symptoms of stress such as muscle tension are cured or can be avoided by learning how to balance your neck properly.

PILATES
Used by many dancers, this technique combines breathing methods with exercises and improved posture work. Many of the movements are very small, but they exercise the muscles deeply. When you begin, a Pilates teacher will give you an assessment to determine what might need correcting.

CHINESE WAND WORKOUT
A distant relative of t'ai chi, involving postures for balancing the body and mind. In addition, a practitioner also holds a four foot (approx. one metre) bamboo cane or wooden stick. By looking at the way you hold the wand, a teacher is able to see if you have any postural problems.

T'AI CHI
Originating in China and developed as a combative martial art, t'ai chi is mainly practised nowadays as a spiritual and physical fitness regime. It is centred around the Taoist beliefs of balancing yin and yang – dark and light energies – within the body. By circulating energy around the body, stress is reduced and well-being ensured.

Natural

Ther

Natural therapies have a crucial role in relieving stress. Here, we explain how these therapies can help you improve your general health and energy levels:

- get to know what a range of therapies involve and what they can be used for
- give yourself simple acupressure treatment
- discover the benefits of aromatherapy
- feel the benefits a massage will bring – to yourself or someone else
- learn about the power of crystals

Therapies

Choosing natural therapy

There are so many types of natural therapy available today – but how do you choose the one that's right for you? This section looks at some of the therapies currently available. Most of them are holistic – which means that they treat the whole person, rather than just specific problems or illnesses, as conventional Western medicine does. They aim to make you fitter, healthier and happier – as well as symptom-free.

When you choose a practitioner, make sure you check their qualifications with a professional body. For help with this, see the Useful Contacts section at the back of this book. If you are going to be working with the practitioner more than once or twice, it is also important that you feel a warm rapport with them. A good way of choosing a practitioner is through personal recommendation – although what worked well for a friend may not necessarily be right for you.

Don't forget the most obvious port of call – your family doctor. He or she is the first stop in looking after your health and if you any have worries about your health you should always contact them first. They may also be able to refer you to a suitable complementary practitioner.

If you feel talking to someone about your life would be of benefit, consider visiting a psychotherapist.

There are many different schools of therapy to choose from, ranging from psychoanalysis to much shorter, more focused therapy which looks at how you can alter your behaviour to combat stress. Life coaches are also gaining in popularity and can best be likened to personal trainers for the mind. Unlike therapists, they do not look at the root causes of your problems but on the changes you want to make to your life and how to carry them out.

The treatments mentioned in this section include some which you can do yourself and some where qualified practitioners assess and treat you. Even those which you can do yourself often work more effectively when you see a practitioner first. For instance, an aromatherapist will be able to assess which scents are right for you – then allowing you to continue the treatment in the comfort of your own home.

ACUPRESSURE

Acupressure helps relieve stress, boosts your immune system and strengthens the flow of energy around the body. In acupressure, body energy is directly manipulated by working on a system of points and meridians. The meridians are the pathways where the vital energy flows through the body and the points are places where you can tap into that energy.

   For a proper acupressure treatment, you should consult a qualified practitioner. You can try this short and simple treatment yourself, however, to help improve your stress relief, concentration and memory. Using the fingers, apply pressure to the points indicated on the diagram below for between one to three minutes, either massaging or rubbing them. Repeat daily.

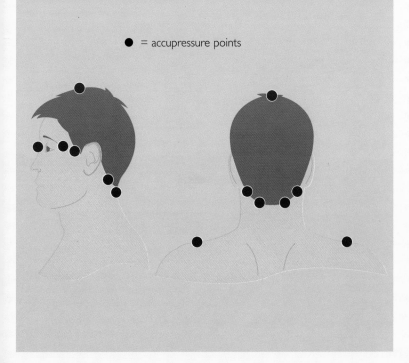

● = accupressure points

Popular treatments

Are you confused about what natural therapies involve? Read on to discover the theories behind these popular treatments.

HOMOEOPATHY

Uses highly diluted, minute quantities of natural substances to cure and prevent both specific illnesses and general lack of good health. Homoeopaths treat the whole person, not just the illness, and a person undergoing homoeopathy will have a thorough consultation to discuss their symptoms, background and personality.

China bark, used as a homoeopathic remedy, is ideal for treating the stresses of trauma and shock.

HYPNOTHERAPY

A hypnotherapist will guide you into a state of trance, in which you are extremely relaxed but retain awareness of your surroundings. You are then helped to explore your problems afresh, with a view to finding suitable solutions.

HERBALISM

Herbal remedies have been relied upon for their healing properties for thousands of years. Even in the West, the use of many herbs, such as ginger or chamomile is commonplace. For treatment of specific illnesses, however, you need to see a qualified herbalist. Chinese herbal remedies are also popular and some are extremely powerful. They should only be used in consultation with a trained practitioner.

ACUPUNCTURE

A relatively painless procedure, acupuncture works on the principle that energy flows through the body but can become blocked, leading to health problems. Needles are inserted into points along the meridian lines of the body in order to unblock the flow.

REIKI

Another therapy based on the idea of energy flow. A Reiki practitioner places his or her hands on the patient with the intent for healing to occur. Energy starts to flow, leading to improved health and wholeness.

SHIATSU

A Japanese technique which uses a mixture of pressure and stretching techniques to stimulate the immune system and the energy flow in the body.

REFLEXOLOGY

Reflexology divides the body into zones, each of which corresponds to an area of the foot. Pressure is exerted on the relevant points on the foot: by unblocking the energy there, reflexology may be used to promote health and prevent specific illnesses occurring.

Which therapy will work for you? Look at the chart below to see whether a particular treatment will be suitable.

	General stress reduction	Strengthens immune system	Psychological problems	Specific illnesses	Practitioner essential
Homoeopathy	✔	✔	✔	✔	✔
Hypnotherapy	◆	✘	✔	✘	✔
Herbalism	◆	✔	◆	✔	✔
Acupuncture	✔	✔	✔	✔	✔
Reiki	✔	✔	✔	✘	✔
Shiatsu	✔	✔	◆	✔	✔
Reflexology	◆	✔	✔	✘	✔
Massage	✔	✔	✔	◆	○

✔ used for this purpose

○ not necessary

◆ infrequently used, or for very specific purposes only

✘ not suitable

51

Aromatherapy

For many thousands of years, people have used the essential oils of flowers, herbs and spices to aid health and relaxation. Aromatherapy is now one of the fastest-growing branches of natural medicine and practitioners recognize the role it can play in promoting health.

Essential oils work in two ways: either by entering the body through the skin when used in massage, or through inhalation when used in an oil-burner or bath.

Oils are usually available both in a ready-to-use diluted form – useful for massage, as well as pure, essential oils. If using pure oils, mix with a carrier or base oil such as almond, using 2–3 drops of essential oil to 5ml of the base. If using an oil burner, put 2–3 drops of oil into the container. A few drops of oil can also be added to your favourite unperfumed cream or lotion. For an aromatherapy bath, add 5–6 drops of oil to fairly hot water, making sure you stay in for 20 minutes to get the effect of the aroma. Breathe deeply and bathe by candlelight for optimum relaxation.

Essential oils should not be applied directly onto the skin and care should be taken to discover whether or not the oils have been pre-diluted with carrier oil. Whichever way you choose to use essential oils, aromatherapy can provide a quick, easy and enjoyable aid to stress relief.

WHICH OIL IS FOR YOU?

Chamomile: soothing and calming; relaxes muscle tension, promotes deep breathing, soothes nerves

Clary sage: relaxing and warming; helpful for PMS and depression; do not use when pregnant

Frankincense: rejuvenating; lifts spirits, fights stress and depression

Juniper: depending on your state of mind, it can either relax or physically stimulate you

Lavender: one of the most useful essential oils.; many uses including insomnia, headaches and anxiety

Lemon: stimulating and refreshing

Orange blossom: soothing, relaxing, releases worries, insomnia

Patchouli: soothing, relaxing; can help to lift your mood

Crystal clear

Crystals have been used all over the world for thousands of years. Ancient traditions often use crystals for prophecy and believe that crystals 'radiate your intention' – so if you have a positive desire, crystals can help it happen.

Many people have discovered that crystals are useful in helping them combat stress. They believe that crystals radiate healing energy, and help the work they are already doing with meditation, yoga, visualization and other stress-relieving practices. Use clear quartz or rose crystal and put a piece prominently in the room where you relax. Cleanse your crystal every few months by leaving it in the sun for 3–4 hours.

Crystals are important in feng shui, where they are hung in the window. Sunlight reflects through them, bringing energy into the house. You can also put crystals near to any electrical equipment – particularly microwaves and computers. They soak up harmful frequencies which can affect concentration, disturb sleep and damage our immune systems.

A thoroughly up-to-date method of using crystals is known as 'electro-crystal therapy'. With this technique, invented in 1983, the body is rebalanced by pulsing it with electromagnetic waves which have passed through coloured crystals. The practitioner photographs the patient's energy field, which helps in diagnosing particular areas and problems to be treated. Crystal-filled electrodes are then placed over the areas which are emitting negative energies to pulse balancing frequencies into them.

Electro-crystal therapy can be used to treat a range of health and stress problems, particularly exhaustion and sleeping difficulties.

Place a clear quartz crystal in a window where it can catch the sunlight.

Healing hands

Massage is an excellent way of combatting stress. It helps you bolster your immune system, relieves the tension accumulated in your body, breaks down the toxins held in your body and improves your posture and body awareness. Psychologically, it improves the spirits, gives comfort and boosts energy.

To give or receive a massage, make sure that you have created a relaxing and private environment, with soft or concealed lighting. The room should be kept pleasantly warm. You will need a futon, thin mattress, or massage table to lie on, plenty of towels to cover the body, and oil to aid the massage process.

Probably the best massage for a beginner to perform is the whole-back massage, a procedure which takes around 15–20 minutes. The masseuse should start with strokes called 'effleurage' – long, sweeping strokes using the flat of the hand. The pressure should be smooth and flowing. Move up and down the length of the back, before going on to the sides of the body. Then stroke over the shoulders and the neck, continuing the movements over the head.

Next, fan the hands up the sides of the spine and down the side of the body to relax the muscles. Follow this with circular hand movements, keeping one hand flat on the body, stroking the other hand around it. Then repeat the effleurage strokes. Knead the sides of the body, using a deeper hand pressure, and follow this with kneading movements over the shoulder blades and up to the back of the neck.

Using long strokes up the sides of the spine, press upwards using the thumbs. Massage the sacrum (base of the spine area) using firm strokes.

Finish with further effleurage strokes, and then some very light, feathery strokes. Allow the receiver to lie still for a few moments to recover.

SELF-MASSAGE

Try massaging your own face to help ease stress:

- pinching together your thumbs and forefingers, gently squeeze your eyebrows, moving all the way down the sides of your face
- squeeze the bridge of your nose with one hand, then press your thumbs down both sides of your nose
- with your forefinger, press around your upper lip and down to your chin
- stretch your tongue inside your mouth and move your jaw around
- pinch the sides of your jaw and neck, finishing off with long, comforting strokes over your entire head and hair

Feel better

Feel

Finally, here are some quick and easy ways of calming down – right now. Try to use them regularly, and they will become a second-nature mechanism for when the going gets rough. This section includes:

- twenty ways to reduce stress in an instant
- relaxation techniques to still your body and mind
- and how to create a bedtime routine which will help you sleep like a baby

now better

Instant calm

You're very stressed – and you need to calm down immediately. Hard day at work, children driving you crazy, house in a mess? Try one of these quick and easy ways to relieve your stress right now.

- Play music – but it's got to be the right sort. Soothing classical music is excellent. Or try an ambient-style CD which will have music specifically chosen for its relaxing or uplifting qualities.
- Pop a sheet of bubble-wrap.
- Squeeze a hand exerciser or soft juggling ball.
- If you live or work in a noisy area, buy some earplugs.
- Have a laugh – try watching a comic film.
- Get out into nature. Try gardening or walking.

Whether you have a large garden or a window box, gardening is a good way to relieve stress.

- Try a remedy from the *Bach Flower* range, available from good chemists and health stores. Each remedy is a mixture of flowers and small amounts of alcohol, taken in small amounts on the tongue or in water. They are symptom specific, such as *Mimulus*, which is recommended for fear. *Rescue Remedy* is the most popular, combining five of the most beneficial flowers and useful for all stressful occasions. You can also add 10 drops to your bath.
- Have a nap.
- Stroke your pet cat or dog. Research has shown that this reduces your heart rate – but it's probably best not to try it with the goldfish, though!
  - Go floating – a trip to a flotation tank centre can be a delicious and exciting treat. All you do is slip into a darkened tank filled with warm, salted water, where you simply lie back and float on the water. Half an hour in the dark, perhaps with calming music, will help to keep your problems in perspective.

- Take some time out from working at your computer – say 15 minutes.
- Switch off your mobile phone.
- Make a list of things to do, and put down realistic times for when you can achieve them. If you are able to delete anything from your list, then do so.
- Run around the block.
- Do some vigorous housework. You'll work off your tension and have a much cleaner house into the bargain.
- Pound some pillows, making as much noise as possible.
- Have a sauna.
- Try some aromatherapy.
- Clear out a junk-filled cupboard.
- To lift your spirits instantly, if you can afford to, buy yourself a little treat.

Soothing aromatherapy oils are the perfect way to calm down your body. Choose a suitable oil, such as relaxing patchouli, light your burner and simply unwind (see also page 52).

QUALITY TIME

Time to yourself can be hard to find when there's work, family, partner or friends to worry about but it's essential in order to feel relaxed, gather your thoughts and prepare for the next onslaught.

Arrange certain times that are reserved for you alone. Ask your partner, friends or family to look after your children, if necessary. If your (older) children are being demanding, shut yourself in your bedroom and let them get on with it. Putting smaller children in front of a video while you have a cup of tea is not going to harm them – and may do you the world of good.

And, while you may crave each other's company after a working day, make sure the children go to bed early enough for there to be time which is adults-only. Both you and they will benefit if you are more relaxed.

Total relaxation

Here are some simple techniques to make your whole body relax – and some of them can even be done at your desk! Practice these techniques as often as possible.

- Clench, then let go, each group of muscles. Start with your toes and work up to your head.

- Try a yoga breathing technique: shut one nostril, breathe in through the other one and count to eight. Shut the other nostril with your other thumb, release the first nostril and breathe out to the count of eight. Repeat several times.

- When you have eye-strain, stop what you are doing immediately. Press the heels of your hands gently into your eyes and breathe deeply for one minute.

- Use positive self-talk and some simple affirmations:
    I am totally relaxed.
    My life is great right now.
    Energy is flowing through my body.

SLEEP

A good night's sleep is essential to physical and mental health, but one of the side-effects of stress is often insomnia – whether it's waking up in the early hours worrying, or the inability to fall asleep in the first place.

- You can create an atmosphere where sleep is more likely. Have an evening routine which helps you wind down, by reading a book or listening to peaceful music.

- To relax your mind and body before sleep, and to help you switch off from the events of the day: lie down, shut your eyes, and place one hand on your diaphragm. Imagine healing light passing through one nostril, going through your body and then out of the other nostril.

- Make sure your bedroom is comfortable but try not to work or eat in it.

- Aromatherapy – either through massage or in your bath – before bed can be helpful. Try lavender, neroli, sandalwood or ylang-ylang essential oils.

- Try to go to bed and get up at the same time every day, regardless of how much sleep you've had, and try not to nap during the day. This will set-up a continuous routine for your body.

- Use meditation to still your thoughts as part of your bedtime routine. Milky drinks or chamomile or valerian tea are especially soothing and can help you sleep.

- Try not to exercise less than 4 hours before bed, as you will find calming down in order to sleep more difficult. Avoid drinking tea or coffee after 6 p.m., or falling asleep on the sofa.

- If you have chronic insomnia, then visit your doctor: it could be sign of depression.

Storing lavender in your linen cupboard or sprinkling a couple of drops of lavender oil on your sheets will instantly calm you, creating a beautifully fragranced and relaxing atmosphere, perfect for sleep.

Useful contacts

The following organizations will be able to supply you with information and equipment on all aspects of stress relief:

In the UK

Acupuncture Council
63 Jeddo Road
London W12 9HQ
Tel: 44 (0)20 8735 0400
Fax: 44 (0)20 8735 0404
www.acupuncture.org.uk

Alcohol Concern
40 Copperfield Street
London SE1 0EE
Tel: 44 (0)20 7928 7377
Fax: 44 (0)20 7928 4644

Body Control Pilates Association
Tel: 44 (0)870 169 0000

British Acupuncture Council
Park House, 206–208 Latimer Road
London W10 6RE
Tel: 44 (0)20 8 964 0222

British Association for Counselling
1 Regent Place, Rugby
Warwickshire CV21 4UH
Tel: 44 (0)1788 578328

British Homoeopathic Association
27a Devonshire Street
London W1N 1RJ
Tel: 44 (0)20 7935 2163
www.nhsconfed\bha

British Wheel of Yoga
1 Hamilton Place, Boston Road
Sleaford, Lincolnshire NG34 7ES
Tel: 44 (0)1529 306851
Fax: 44 (0)1529 303233
www.members.aol.com/wheelyoga

Chinese Wand Association
91 Colby Road, Thurmaston
Leicester LE4 8LG
(send SAE for groups in your area)

Institute for Optimum Nutrition
13 Blades Court, Deodar Road
London SW15 2NU
Tel: 44 (0)20 8877 9993
Fax: 44 (0)20 8877 9980

Council for Complementary and Alternative Medicine
63 Jeddo Road
London W12 9HQ
Tel: 44 (0)20 8735 0632

National Federation of Spiritual Healers
Old Manor Farm Studio, Church Street
Sunbury-on-Thames
Middlesex TW16 6RG
Tel: 44 (0)981 616080

National Register of Hypnotherapists
12 Cross Street, Nelson
Lancashire BB9 7EN
Tel: 44 (0)1282 699 378

**National Register of Personal
Fitness Trainers**
Thornton House, Thornton Road
London SW19 4NG
Tel: 44 (0)20 8944 6688
Fax: 44 (0)20 8944 0353

School of Meditation
158 Holland Park Avenue
London W11 4UH
Tel: 44 (0)20 7603 6116

Smoking Quitline
Tel: 44 (0)800 00 22 00
www.ash.org.uk

School of Electro Crystal Therapy
117 Long Drive, South Ruislip
Middlesex HA4 0HL
(send SAE for groups in your area)

**Society of Teachers of the
Alexander Technique**
20 London House, 266 Fulham Road
London SW10 9EL
Tel: 44 (0)20 7351 08287

T'ai Chi UK
Tel: 44 (0)20 7407 4775
www.taichi.co.uk

UK Council for Psychotherapy
167-169 Great Portland Street
London W1N 5FB
Tel: 44 (0)20 7436 3002

In the US
Californian School of Herbal Studies
PO Box 39, Forestville
California 95436
Tel: 1 707 88 7457

**Iyengar Yoga National Association
of the United States**
Tel: 1 800 889 9642
www.comnet.org/iynaus
Provides details of membership,
teachers and events.

National Centre for Homoeopathy
801 N Fairfax Street
Alexandria
VA 22314
Tel: 1 703 548 7790

In Australia
**Australian Natural Therapists
Association**
PO Box 522, Sutherland
NSW 2232
Tel: 61 (02) 521 2063

**National Herbalists' Association
of Australia**
PO Box 65, Kingsgrove
NSW 2208
Tel: 61 (02) 787 4523

Index